Little Learning Labs

UNOFFICIAL MINECRAFT FOR KIDS

**26 Family-Friendly
Creative Building Activities
That Teach Math, Science,
History, and Culture**

**JOHN MILLER AND
CHRIS FORNELL SCOTT**

To my wife Audrey, for believing in me. — JM

**To the child in all of us who isn't afraid of where new adventures might lead.
To my sons, Josiah, Eli, and Finn. You inspire me.** — CFS

Brimming with creative inspiration, how-to projects, and useful information to enrich your everyday life, Quarto Knows is a favorite destination for those pursuing their interests and passions. Visit our site and dig deeper with our books into your area of interest: Quarto Creates, Quarto Cooks, Quarto Homes, Quarto Lives, Quarto Drives, Quarto Explores, Quarto Gifts, or Quarto Kids.

Inspiring | Educating | Creating | Entertaining

MIX
Paper from responsible sources
FSC® C104723

© 2018 Quarto Publishing Group USA Inc.
Text © 2016 Quarto Publishing Group USA Inc.

First Published in 2018 by Quarry Books, an imprint of The Quarto Group,
100 Cummings Center, Suite 265-D, Beverly, MA 01915, USA.
T (978) 282-9590 F (978) 283-2742 QuartoKnows.com

All rights reserved. No part of this book may be reproduced in any form without written permission of the copyright owners. All images in this book have been reproduced with the knowledge and prior consent of the artists concerned, and no responsibility is accepted by producer, publisher, or printer for any infringement of copyright or otherwise, arising from the contents of this publication. Every effort has been made to ensure that credits accurately comply with information supplied. We apologize for any inaccuracies that may have occurred and will resolve inaccurate or missing information in a subsequent reprinting of the book.

Quarry Books titles are also available at discount for retail, wholesale, promotional, and bulk purchase. For details, contact the Special Sales Manager by email at specialsales@quarto.com or by mail at The Quarto Group, Attn: Special Sales Manager, 401 Second Avenue North, Suite 310, Minneapolis, MN 55401, USA.

10 9 8 7 6 5 4 3 2 1

ISBN: 978-1-63159-561-5

Digital edition published in 2018
The content in this book originally appeared in the book *Unofficial Minecraft Lab for Kids* (Quarry Books, 2016).

Design: Kathie Alexander

NOT AN OFFICIAL MINECRAFT PRODUCT. NOT APPROVED BY OR ASSOCIATED WITH MOJANG.
Printed in China

Contents

Introduction: Notes for Parents and Teachers

In an age where games have multimillion-dollar budgets, high-end computer graphics, and Hollywood-inspired storylines, how can a game that comes with no instructions, no clear goals, and no-frills blocky graphics become a mega-hit widely lauded for its creative and immersive play?

Perhaps it's because players walk away from a Minecraft session with a deep sense of fulfillment and are highly motivated to return and improve their skills. Minecraft challenges them to explore a new, unlimited world and interact with other players and the environment. They mine for resources and craft tools that they use to modify their environment to fit their needs. Or perhaps it's because Minecraft is versatile and highly adaptable to any player at any experience level and has something to teach everyone. Its open-ended nature provides rich opportunities for exploration and discovery and satisfies a natural inquisitiveness while promoting detailed and deep conversations, both in and out of the game.

Adults might assume that playing Minecraft is just like playing any other video game, but kids know that Minecraft offers much more than entertainment. As kids become experts in Minecraft, they create a knowledge gap that is often difficult for adults to bridge. Players can speak the language of Minecraft while nonplayers may be confused.

This book bridges that gap. It's designed for adults who want to connect with their Minecraft players by improving their understanding of the game and by extending their child's learning with both in- and out-of-game activities. It employs analog (community) connections that encourage kids to interact with the adults in their lives. New conversations and paths of creativity will reveal themselves as you complete both the in-game and out-of-game portions of the individual labs and the quests (a set of two labs). In some instances, you'll help the Minecraft expert with the analog connections, and at other times, the game expert will teach you how to build in-game portions of the lab.

WHAT CAN MINECRAFT TEACH?

Minecraft encourages players to create, share, and innovate as no other game has ever done before. It promotes continuous learning. Teaching and learning from others is as much a part of the game as building a shelter or fighting creepers. While playing in creative mode, with an unlimited supply of every block in their inventory available, players have the freedom to explore their imagination. Players monitor their inventories, conduct ongoing needs assessments, and consider options to expand and improve their character's status in the game. By learning more skills and discovering or crafting more resources, players better prepare themselves for each day, and the reward for their hard work is enhanced playability. When playing in survival mode, players must rely upon a varied and changing set of skills to achieve their immediate and long-term goals.

Minecraft encourages numerous positive traits and builds life skills and spatial understanding. Players develop problem-solving strategies for surviving each night while setting and prioritizing goals for the next day. Food is important, but so is shelter. Armor and weapons will help fight off mobs but require specific and often hard-to-find resources and crafting. It is only through perseverance and planning that players will be successful.

Further, players value the craftsmanship and skills of others while sharing knowledge and innovations, especially in creative multiplayer mode. They develop large-scale, imaginative, team-oriented projects and break down tasks to assign pieces to players based on skill sets. This interdependence builds positive relationships and flexible thinkers.

The vast amount of creative and humorous storytelling and adventure sharing online reflects Minecraft's popularity. Thousands of websites and YouTube videos are dedicated to design tutorials, building, and gameplay strategies. Survival tips, creative ideas, and answers to player questions are only a click or two away on the Internet. Younger players follow and often imitate their favorite YouTube stars, producing and sharing videos and tutorials of their own and emulating a business model for the twenty-first century.

MINECRAFT IN SCHOOLS

Educators are using Minecraft as a tool for learning in most grade levels and content areas in classrooms around the world, and have discovered that their students are excited to share their expertise as they use a favorite game.

The game's encouragement of sharing ideas and seeking help via a thriving and popular Google Group energizes educators as well. Some teachers create and share Minecraft worlds and the associated lesson plans that target specific concepts, skills, and units of study. Some worlds come complete with buildings and nonplayer characters ready for students to explore and interact with. Other teachers design worlds for focused student or team collaboration and task students with building out the world to meet content objectives.

The scale of every block in Minecraft represents 1 cubic meter, so applications in mathematics and geometry are clear. Students can visualize concepts such as area, perimeter, and volume in three dimensions; demonstrate ratio, proportion, and fractions; and collect and graph data, all in the game world. Science teachers can use Minecraft to teach geology, physics, and biology. Students are aptly creating models of plate tectonics, DNA, animal cells, and even quantum behavior. Redstone blocks in Minecraft release a power source that students and teachers can use to explore electrical circuitry and operate switches, pistons, and logic gates. One popular modification teaches computer programming, while another supports environmental education.

Minecraft is also great for teaching social sciences and literacy. Students demonstrate their understanding of setting, plot, theme, and conflict by recreating children's stories and young adult novels scene by scene. Books and journals within the game can support student- and teacher-generated text and can include live links to information available on the Internet.

Historical figures can come alive and interact with students in ways traditional textbooks cannot. By role-playing with characters from history, students can experience the wonders of ancient Greece or explore a Civil War battlefield and then reflect on their adventures through journal writing and interactions with each other.

HOW TO USE THIS BOOK

Each of the two labs within the six quests has both an in-game and an out-of-game activity, which is called the "family activity." Most labs suggest doing the out-of-game activities first as a way to research and prepare for in-game building.

You can either work through the labs sequentially, or you can bounce from one lab to another. If you're new to Minecraft, consider starting at the beginning, as Quest 1 introduces basic gameplay. You can also use the labs to connect your child's love of the game with an out-of-game learning experience. For example, if you're planning to visit a museum, consider skipping to Quest 4, The Arts, whose labs are a perfect fit for that experience. Quest 6, however, is best left until you've completed most, if not all, of the other labs, as it's a culmination of your work in the book.

Use this book as a bridge between Minecraft players (usually kids) and their nonplayer counterparts (typically parents or teachers). Sit down with your children and pick a place to start. We want this book to open and build communication, collaboration, creativity, and critical thinking between kids and adults. Nonplayers will learn about Minecraft, while players will enjoy learning about analog, community, and other out-of-game connections.

We encourage you to start building in Minecraft with your kids to further develop your bond. Minecraft naturally offers opportunities to try, fail, and try again. Use those same principles as you work on the out-of-game part of each lab.

MINECRAFT BASICS

What Is Minecraft? Minecraft is a game. Yet, since its inception in 2009, it has evolved into an amazing tool for creating, innovating, teaching, and learning. It absorbs players in a blocky, three-dimensional world where they are free to explore and create whatever they can think of using a simple interface. With over 150 million copies sold, it is one of the world's all-time best-selling games.

Minecraft is a unique game in that there are no levels that you pass to continue on inside the game. The game is open-ended, where you create the experience for yourself as you play. The basics of playing Minecraft encourage collaboration and not

competition. Certainly players can turn the game into a competitive experience, by playing player versus player (PvP) or racing through a parkour map. When playing in "survival" mode, players gain experience (XP) in a variety of skills.

Single Player vs. Multiplayer

You can play Minecraft alone or with others; and there's no difference in the in-game mechanics between the two. Purchasing a Minecraft account allows players to play in either mode, but it also depends on the platform (see page 8). All players must have their own license and, generally, their own copy of the game for the platform they are using. Some exceptions include console editions.

Playing in single player mode is a solitary yet interactive experience commonly used by players to hone their skills or develop worlds or maps without the potential for interruption from others. Individuals can open or otherwise share their worlds at any time with other players.

In multiplayer mode, players interact with each other, oftentimes collaborating to achieve common goals and develop strategies for expansion and resource accumulation. Through cooperative play and experimentation, players polish their skills in areas like redstone mining, building, and food production. Compared to most other games, Minecraft removes the arguing often associated with playing collaboratively.

Creative Mode and Survival Mode

Players must decide between two common game mode options when beginning a new game: creative mode and survival mode. (You may hear players talk about a third option for play known as adventure mode. This mode preserves structures and special modifications and limits destructive behaviors or "griefing" [see "Learn to Speak Minecraft," page 10] from visitors to the map.)

In "creative" mode, every player has access to an unlimited supply of blocks of every kind. They can fly high in the air and dive deep under water without fear of dying. Players cannot harm others or be killed or attacked by mobs; they don't need to eat or worry about their health. They can concentrate instead on creating whatever their minds can think of. When playing in this mode with others, builds can reach epic proportions.

When first playing in "survival" mode, players quickly discover that they need to feed themselves and avoid falls from high places to stay healthy. Loss of health due to hunger or physical activity will eventually lead to death. They will also discover that when nighttime comes, they are susceptible to attack by monsters like zombies and creepers.

Players in survival mode begin play with nothing and, through exploration of their environment, gather resources like wood and stone. They then craft these blocks into tools, weapons, and other useful items. They must construct a shelter to keep the monsters out at night and acquire food by killing animals or harvesting seeds and growing crops. As days and nights pass, players become more proficient at gathering resources and crafting items. Weapons and armor protect players from monsters, allowing them to travel at night and explore more of their unique world.

How to Play

This section references the default keystrokes and mouse options for playing Minecraft on a PC. This is the version most adults favor. You can find instructions and commands for other platforms by searching Minecraft.gamepedia.com.

Minecraft does not come with any directions or instructions. After launching the game for the first time and selecting creative or survival mode, you appear at a random location in a randomly generated world. That's it. You must figure out the rest—which is what most kids do. They voraciously consume information about the game and its features by watching hours of YouTube videos, reading page after page of tips and strategies on the web, and comparing notes with their friends while playing.

It's our hope that you engage your children's passion for learning everything they can about Minecraft and ask them to become your teacher or mentor. We designed our labs to showcase their expertise yet keep you in a comfortable place as a learner.

VERSIONS AND PLATFORMS

Minecraft was originally developed as a game for the PC, but it's now available in several versions and can be played on multiple platforms. See the list below to discover the similarities and differences among the various platforms and versions.

It's important to note that worlds and maps created using one platform may not be playable in a different platform, and that in order to play with others in multiplayer mode, all players need to be using the same platform *and* version.

	PC PLATFORM	CONSOLE	POCKET EDITION PE
OPERATING SYSTEM OR DEVICE	Windows, Mac, Linux	Xbox, PlayStation, WiiU	Android, iOS, Windows 10 Windows Phone
FEATURES	The original, full version of Minecraft containing all blocks, special features, and craftable items	A mostly full-featured, earlier version of the original	An abridged version of the original designed for the limitations of small touchscreens
MULTIPLAYER?	Yes, full integration	Yes, available via the Xbox or PlayStation network	Yes, via local network or online PE server
KEY LIMITATIONS	None	Limits to world size, number of players, and player skins	Crafting options; no hunger or other dimensions

Playing in multiplayer mode means that all the players in your group will need to join one Minecraft server. There are two options available for this:

- Connect with each other through a Local Area Network (LAN). One player starts the world, selects the option to open it to a LAN, and receives an address to share with other players. The other players launch Minecraft and type in this address to join the game.

- Connect through one of numerous online servers, which usually require a monthly fee to join. Minecraft.net offers a hosted option known as Minecraft Realms at a modest price and is a good choice for family play. You connect to an online server in similar fashion to a LAN—sign up for the service and connect to it through the Minecraft launcher.

Lesson 1: Small Steps

You don't need to know everything about this game before you play it. Enjoy the time you spend playing Minecraft with the young ones in your life and be open to their guidance. We suggest playing for the first time in survival mode. Ask your young teacher to set the world to peaceful so that monsters are not active. This will give you more time to practice.

1. After launching the game, press W to move forward.
2. Press A to slide to the left.
3. Press D to slide to the right
4. Press S to take a step backward.
5. Tap the spacebar to hop in the air. If there is a block in front of you, press W *and* spacebar to jump on top of it.
6. If you are playing in creative mode, double tap the spacebar and you will fly in the air. Hold down the spacebar and press W at the same time to fly up and forward.
7. Press and hold the shift button to land.

There are numerous options for customizing each player's controls. Beginners should stick with the basic movement keys of W, A, S, and D.

Lesson 2: Movement

The mouse is used to control where your head is looking. Move the mouse left to look left. Move it right to look right. Now let's try some combinations.

1. Press and hold W *while* moving the mouse to the left. You'll travel forward several steps to the left.
2. Repeat, but move to the right now. You'll travel forward several steps to the right.

Lesson 3: Breaking and Placing Blocks

By now, you'll have discovered that objects are likely blocking your path. You'll use the two buttons on your mouse to first break and then place blocks. You can break and place blocks up to five blocks away. You can't break or place any blocks directly beneath you without hopping first.

1. Find a tree or block of sand or soil, walk up to it, and look directly at the block. Aim the tiny crosshairs (+) at the block and hold down the left click button on your mouse until the block breaks.
2. Move forward and the block will pop into one of your inventory slots (on the tool belt) at the bottom of the screen. Break several more blocks until you get the hang of it.
3. Now let's place a block. Put a block in your right hand by selecting the number of the slot in your inventory that corresponds to the block. You have nine slots in your tool belt.
4. Locate a spot where you would like to place that block, line up the crosshairs, and right-click.

Lesson 4: Inventory

You've now learned how to move, jump on top of blocks, and break and place blocks. To return to the settings screen, press the ESC key. This is where you quit the game. Press ESC again to go back to the game.

1. Now press E to see your inventory. If you are playing in survival mode, you'll discover the blocks you have mined are located in your tool belt, but you'll also see more available slots above the original nine. This is your backpack area. Drag and drop a few blocks from your tool belt to the backpack. Blocks stored in your backpack are always available by pressing E.
2. If you are playing in creative mode, you'll discover that you have access to *all* the Minecraft blocks. Scroll through your inventory and click on the tabs to see all of the blocks and items. Drag blocks you wish to place into your tool belt for easy access.

Congratulations! You now have enough information to explore your new world. Once you've gotten the basics, you can customize your controls. When you are ready to learn more, visit Minecraftopia. com for information, tips, and crafting recipes.

Learn to Speak Minecraft

It may appear that Minecraft players are speaking a language of their own. Here are a few key terms explained.

Bedrock: Everyone loves digging in Minecraft, but eventually you'll hit bottom. Bedrock is the bottom layer—you cannot break bedrock in survival mode.

Biome: Every Minecraft world has multiple biomes, or ecological regions. Fly around enough in creative mode and you will come across deserts, mountain ranges, oceans, jungles, and many others.

Crafting table: Players use a crafting table to "craft" or create artifacts used in the game.

Creeper: An especially sneaky monster that loves to waddle up next to you and explode.

The End: You can play Minecraft in a sort of sequential order. You begin with nothing in survival mode, become powerful through experience and by crafting resources and then, if you still need a challenge, a final battle against a dragon awaits in another dimension known as The End.

Enderman: A tall, dark, skinny monster that will leave you alone—unless you look into its purple eyes.

Griefer/Griefing: Some players like to join a multiplayer server and sneak around, destroy stuff, and take your things. These are griefers. Nobody likes griefers.

Mobs: These are all the creatures you'll discover while playing Minecraft. There are friendly mobs such as chickens and sheep, neutral mobs like Enderman, and hostile mobs like creepers, zombies, and skeletons.

Mods: The creative team behind Minecraft have opened up the game to other developers by allowing them to create modifications to the original game. These are mostly free and change the game by adding new features or modifying existing ones.

Nether: You can access this scary underworld by building a special portal.

PvP (Player vs. Player): When playing with this feature enabled, players may harm and even kill each other. There is a widely popular Minecraft mini-game based on the popular book series *The Hunger Games*.

Redstone: A special block in Minecraft that releases dust when broken and can be used to provide power to crafted items like pistons and automated doors.

Skin: The fashionable outfit that your character is wearing. Skins are highly customizable in the PC version of Minecraft. Visit minecraftskins.com for hundreds of examples.

Spawn: This is the location where everyone will initially arrive in a new world. Your spawn point changes once you create a home with a bed and lay in it. When you die in survival mode, you will respawn at this point.

Steve: The generic character everyone begins life as. Mojang, the company that created the game, has recently allowed players to choose between Steve and Alex, a female character.

World: When you create a new game, Minecraft generates a unique world for you to play in. You can save, delete, or share worlds with others.

SHARING LABS AND QUESTS

Sharing builds is integral to the Minecraft experience. Here are some suggestions on how and where to share Minecraft creations.

YouTube

Here are some ways to make a successful video for YouTube:

Edit the video. YouTube has a decent video editor built into the platform. Go to YouTube.com/editor. From the editor you can clip sections, add music and text, and even annotate the videos. Annotations are clickable pop-up boxes that allow viewers to subscribe or be redirected to an outside website.

Choose the music. Most music is copyrighted and not free to reuse or add to your video. In the YouTube video editor, you can access free music to add to your videos. Of course, you can always create your own music.

Would you watch it? One of the best benchmarks for good videos is to ask yourself, "Would I watch it?" This simple question is quite powerful. You watched the video as you edited it, but would you watch the video if you didn't know who had created it? If you're not sure, upload your video and make it unlisted. Share your unlisted video with other family and friends to get feedback.

Video settings. Choose your visibility setting when uploading your videos. YouTube gives three choices: public, unlisted, and private. Public videos are easily searchable by anyone online, unlisted videos are not searchable but can be easily shared with the video link, and private videos can only be viewed by you.

Allow or disallow comments. If you are making videos public and are concerned about negative comments, consider leaving comments off. Under your channel, select the video you've uploaded. You can control whether viewers can leave comments. Go to advanced settings to find the option to turn off comments. It's also possible to review comments before they are posted.

Tag your video. Use the hashtag #minecrafterbook as you share and publish your work online. We love to see what you create in and out of Minecraft. Tweet @minecrafterbook and we'll retweet your work. Using hashtags and Twitter handles will help build a community of people working through the quests and labs.

Screencasting

Screencasting is how your favorite YouTubers record their gameplay. The screencasting tool is different for every device you play on. There are several free or inexpensive options for screencasting for PC and tablets. It's a little different if you want to record from a console. Here's a list:

Windows/Mac. Camtasia: $, Adobe Captivate: $$$; Screencast-O-Matic: free

Tablet. Between the time of writing and publishing, there will likely be even more apps available. We suggest doing a search for "screencasting" or "record screen."

Console. To record on a console you need to buy an extra piece of hardware. The devices go by a couple of different names: GameDVR and Game Capture. Both terms will get you the same device. The device is installed between the console and screen.

Screenshots

Screenshots are pictures of the device screen. Every device has a way of snapping a picture of what is on the screen. We've listed some examples of how to grab a screenshot below; please note that your device may be different.

PC. Press F2 to grab a screenshot inside the game. Once the screenshot is taken you'll see text in the chat area that lets you know the filename. To find the screenshots on a Windows machine, go to %appdata%\.minecraft\screenshots. On a Mac, go to Library/Application Support/minecraft/screenshots.

Tablet. For Apple products, press and hold both the home and the power buttons simultaneously. The image is saved in your camera roll. Android varies based on the operating system. Typically, hold the down volume key and the power button at the same time. The screenshot will be saved in the gallery.

Console. For Xbox, double tap the Xbox button, then the Y button. For PlayStation, press and hold the share button for at least one second.

QUEST 1

Using Your Inventory

In this quest, you'll be using many of the blocks in your inventory. Start with the basics and strengthen your skills.

LAB 1

DO YOU MINE?
Learn the basics of gameplay while gathering resources.
Enjoy a Minecraft-themed scavenger hunt outside of the game.

LAB 2

FIRE WHEN READY!
Send marshmallows flying before creating a TNT-powered cannon
to knock down a castle wall.

Do You Mine?

There's no right way to play Minecraft. It's a sandbox game—meaning that it's open-ended rather than structured—where players are free to explore, mine, and craft their experiences.

The act of mining is one of the key activities in Minecraft, and looking for the right blocks, or materials, can sometimes feel like a digital scavenger hunt. In the family activity, you'll hunt for real-life versions of items you'll find inside the game.

Crafting is the second key activity of the game. For the Minecraft part of this lab, you'll use resources you mine to craft useful items to make living and crafting more fun. You'll start at the beginning by punching trees and move toward crafting tools and a shelter, which is how everyone starts playing.

Family Activity: Scavenger Hunt

A scavenger hunt is a fun way to get your hands dirty while looking for the items on the list. Be sure to work together, as some of the items might be difficult to spot.

■ **APPROXIMATE TIME TO COMPLETE**
   45 minutes

■ **MATERIALS**
   Scavenger Hunt Checklist
      (see page 133 for the complete list)
   Timer

1. Share the scavenger hunt list on page 73 with your team. Consider how you can work together to tackle the list quickly. This is a time challenge, too!

2. Set the timer for 45 minutes and begin.

3. Once the time is up, add up the number of items you found.

MORE TO EXPLORE
Another way to play: You and your team can keep the list handy during the week and take pictures of the items whenever and wherever you find them. Post the craziest pictures (especially the spider eye) to your blog or social media with the hashtag #minecrafterbook.

SCAVENGER HUNT CHECKLIST

☐ Apple
☐ Bed
☐ Boat
☐ Bow and arrow
☐ Bread
☐ Cactus
☐ Cake
☐ Carpet
☐ Carrot
☐ Coal or charcoal
☐ Cobweb
☐ Compass

☐ Flower pot
☐ Flowers
☐ Furnace
☐ Gold
☐ Glass
☐ Grass
☐ Gravel
☐ Hoe
☐ Ice or snow
☐ Iron
☐ Ladder
☐ Leather
☐ Leaves

☐ Pumpkin pie
☐ Saddle
☐ Sand
☐ Shovel
☐ Sign
☐ Spider eye
☐ Sponge
☐ Stairs
☐ Sticks
☐ Stone
☐ String
☐ Sugar
☐ Tree
☐ Vines

Every block, or material, that's mined in the game has a hardness level that determines which tool is best for breaking it. You can break most blocks by hand, without any tools, but using the right tool will save you lots of time. The general rules of thumb for using tools are shown at right.

Every player starts out with nothing in his or her inventory. The objective is to collect resources to craft a full set of tools so you can mine harder blocks to craft even stronger tools. Once you've collected some blocks, craft new tools and resources to make play even better. Grab a tool and start breaking blocks!

- **GAME MODE**
  Survival

- **APPROXIMATE TIME TO COMPLETE**
  1+ hours in Minecraft

- **PLATFORMS**
  PC/Mac, Consoles, Pocket Edition (PE)

1. **When you first enter the game, you'll start at spawn point. Look around to see what types of resources are nearby. Start mining by punching trees to gather wood.**

2. **Turn the wood you've gathered into a crafting table, which allows you to craft all the tools available in the game (fig. 1). Without a crafting table, you're limited to crafting very few items. It's helpful to have multiple crafting tables. Put one in your house, one in your mineshaft (where the player mines underground for more resources), and one where you're harvesting trees. Start using your crafting table by turning your wood into tools (fig. 2).**

3. **Build a shelter. Your shelter could be on top of a hill made from dirt or inside a mountain surrounded by stone blocks. If you're playing in survival mode, the goal is to build a shelter to protect you from monsters.**

TOOLS CHEAT SHEET

 Axes: for mining and crafting anything made from wood

 Pickaxes: for mining and crafting stone or harder materials

 Shovels: for mining and crafting dirt

 Hoes: for preparing the ground for planting

 Weapons (such as swords): for killing mobs and animals

HARDNESS →

HANDS (NO TOOLS)	WOOD	STONE	IRON	GOLD	DIAMOND

The harder the material a tool is made from, the faster it will break blocks.

Fig. 1: Use the wood you've mined to create a crafting table.

Fig. 2: Use your crafting table and some wood to craft new tools, like the wooden pickaxe shown.

Fig. 3: Build a bed using three blocks of wool and three wood planks.

Fig. 4: Place the bed in a safe place, such as inside your shelter.

Fig. 5: The crafting recipe for a chest.

Fig. 6: Chests are a great place to store extra resources.

4. **Craft a bed, if possible. You'll need three blocks of wool ("mined" from sheep) of any color and three wood planks (fig. 3). Place the bed in a safe place, preferably inside a home (fig. 4). You can break the bed and take it with you when exploring further from home. If you don't make a bed, you can either hide out in your shelter or keep mining and fight any monsters that come your way.**

5. **Crafting a chest (fig. 5) is a great way to keep extra items (fig. 6). Ask your co-player whether crafting a chest is necessary. (In survival mode, players must craft all their resources; if they die, players lose all items in their inventory—unless they have placed them in the chest. In creative mode, players don't need chests, as you can't die and always have access to unlimited items.) Placing two chests next to each other creates one large chest.**

MORE TO EXPLORE

Minecraft was originally called Cave Game. Markus Persson, also known as Notch, started the game with the simple premise of mining to craft. The version you'll play today has more tools, blocks, and resources than any previous version.

Fire When Ready!

In this lab you'll alternate between dodging marshmallows and firing TNT into a medieval fortress. In the family activity, you'll have some fun building a Popsicle stick catapult, while in Minecraft, you'll get acquainted with one of the more popular blocks in your inventory—TNT! TNT is a special block that, when ignited with flint and steel, will explode and destroy blocks located near it (the image above shows an explosion in process). For more details, see the sidebar "Getting to Know TNT in Minecraft," page 20.

■ **APPROXIMATE TIME TO COMPLETE**
30 minutes

■ **MATERIALS**
7 large Popsicle sticks,
6 inches (15 cm) long
10 to 12 rubber bands
Plastic spoon
Marshmallows

Family Activity: Marshmallow Catapult

Fig. 1: These stacked sticks will form the base of the catapult.

Fig. 2: Attach the spoon securely to the end of one stick.

Fig. 3: Attach these two sticks together, making sure to leave one end open.

1. Stack five sticks on top of each other and secure both ends of the stack with rubber bands (fig. 1).

2. Secure the plastic spoon to one of the remaining sticks with at least three rubber bands (fig. 2).

3. Attach the remaining stick beneath the stick with the spoon at the bottom only using a rubber band (fig. 3).

4. Finally, pry open and then slide the end of the launcher around the stack of sticks and securely attach the two components with rubber bands across the center, as shown in figure 4.

5. Load a marshmallow onto your catapult and fire away!

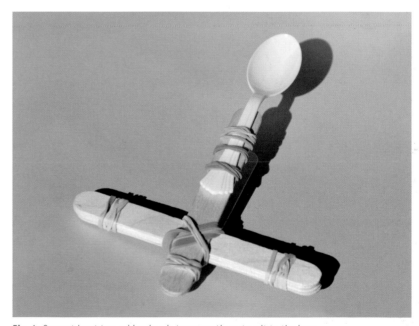

Fig. 4: Cross at least two rubber bands to secure the catapult to the base.

In this part of the lab, you'll build a basic cannon that fires a block of TNT into the distance. The TNT will explode in the air or on the ground. After you've built your first cannon, experiment by adjusting the amount of TNT you use, or build your cannon on the edge of a mountaintop to increase its firing range. See below, right, for more on how TNT works in Minecraft.

Fig. 1: Build two short walls parallel to each other and close off one end.

Fig. 2: Add water to the bottom of the cavity to ensure that the cannon won't explode when the TNT ignites.

GAME MODE

Creative

APPROXIMATE TIME TO COMPLETE

2 hours in Minecraft

PLATFORMS

PC/Mac, Consoles, PE

INVENTORY REQUIREMENTS

Stone blocks
Bucket of water
Lever or button
Redstone wire
Stone slab
Four redstone repeaters
TNT

ONLINE RESOURCE

To see what it would be like to be a human cannonball, check out this YouTube video by DanTDM:
https://goo.gl/4Haq7A

1. Using stone blocks, build two short walls, each one block high and nine blocks long. Build the walls parallel to each other and one block apart. Close off the narrow area between them at one end with another block of stone. The TNT will be launched from the open end (fig. 1).

2. At the closed end of the foundation, place two blocks of stone, one on top of the other. Destroy the block on the bottom (the one touching the ground) and fill the cavity with water. The water should flow all the way to the end of the wall but not beyond it (fig. 2). Adding water to the bottom of the cannon will ensure that it won't explode when the TNT is ignited.

GETTING TO KNOW TNT IN MINECRAFT

Most commonly activated with flint and steel

- Won't destroy blocks under water
- Useful for clearing out large areas
- Use redstone to wire cannons, traps, and other crafty innovations
- Can be placed in a minecart and sent down the rail line as an explosive surprise
- Can be placed next to each other to create colossal explosions

3. Place the lever or button behind the tall block at the closed end of the cannon. Connect the lever to redstone wire. Run the wire along most of the length of both walls. Stop the wire one block short of the end of the wall on the right and two blocks short of the end of the wall on the left (fig. 3).

4. At the open end of the cannon, place the slab on top of the water block and add two more stone blocks to the wall to the left of the slab. Add redstone wire on top of those blocks (fig. 4). These blocks will prime the TNT just before it's launched into the air. When primed, or activated with redstone, TNT blocks blink white.

5. Place four repeaters along the left wall and set the delay on each to at least two ticks (fig. 5). Repeaters slow down the signal from the lever just a bit so the TNT block is launched before it explodes.

6. Make sure the redstone lever is disengaged, then fill the water cavity with TNT blocks (fig. 6). Pull the switch! The blocks of TNT will explode, launching the solitary TNT block at the open end of the cannon into the air.

Fig. 4: Place a slab at the open end, add two blocks to the wall on the left, and run redstone wire on top of the blocks.

Fig. 5: Place four repeaters on the left wall. Set the delay on each to at least two ticks.

Fig. 3: Attach a lever to redstone wire. Run the wire along the walls, stopping it one block from the end of the right wall and two blocks from the end of the left wall.

Fig. 6: Disengage the lever, fill the water cavity with TNT blocks, then pull the switch!

MORE TO EXPLORE

Have each family or team member build a fortress around his or her cannon and see whose can survive the longest. Obsidian is very resistant to explosions. Build and then try to knock down an obsidian tower by firing TNT from multiple cannons.

Textures, Patterns, and Landscapes

In this quest, design a restaurant and create gardens to grow useful crops.

LAB 3

PLEASE BE SEATED
Visit a local restaurant to complete the restaurant research.
In Minecraft, design, craft, and operate a restaurant.

LAB 4

GROW A GARDEN
In Minecraft, prepare the ground, plant seeds, and add water and
some bone meal for the easiest gardening experience. Make real-life
connections by planting seasonal seeds.

Please Be Seated

There are millions of restaurants, big and small, around the world. Restaurants are designed according to the style of food, culture, and community. Patterns and textures exist inside and outside of restaurants. The floor plan for seats, the layout of each dish, even the assembly of food are all patterns.

To complete this lab, the family activity will have you spend time researching local restaurants to explore all their aspects. In the game, you'll craft a restaurant of your own and design it according to your own taste.

 ONLINE RESOURCE

Check out Arch Daily's International Restaurant Design winners:
http://goo.gl/d4v2Mq

Family Activity: Restaurant Research

Researching local restaurants is a fun way to gather crafting inspiration while filling your mental fuel tank for designing your own in Minecraft (see pages 26–27).

■ **APPROXIMATE TIME TO COMPLETE**
   1 hour

■ **MATERIALS**
   Camera
   Notepad and pencil

1. **Choose a restaurant. Consider one that's opened recently or one you've never been to but have wanted to visit.**

2. **While dining in the restaurant, take photographs of the layout. Make notes about patterns and textures. Consider the floor plan, the types of food and how they're served, and even the locations of the bathrooms.**

3. **Visit one or two other restaurants that are larger or smaller than your first one and that serve different cuisines (figs. 1–3). Take photos and make notes. Consider how they're the same as well as how they're different.**

Figs. 1-3: As you research restaurants and their interiors for your in-game design, take note of their patterns and textures.

Designing and building restaurants in the game is an important way to customize your world. It's fun to invite fellow players to visit your restaurant and enjoy a fresh meal of cooked chicken or even a cake.

■ **GAME MODE**
Creative

■ **APPROXIMATE TIME TO COMPLETE**
2–3 hours in Minecraft

■ **PLATFORMS**
PC/Mac, Consoles, PE

1. Sort through the information you gathered in the family activity and choose the elements you would like to include in your restaurant design. Follow the checklist on the opposite page as you design your own. As you work, stay true to your restaurant theme, but also consider doing something surprising.

2. Choose a location for building your restaurant, one that suits its style. Will your restaurant be surrounded by other businesses in a large city? Could your restaurant be on a mountaintop or near a beach? We built a restaurant that blends the indoors with the outdoors (figs. 1 and 2), with a garden next to the seating.

3. The kitchen is the heart of every restaurant. Decide where yours will be in relation to the dining room. The kitchen for this restaurant is in the back, but the food is out front. Think about how many chests you'll need for storage. The furnace cooks food to perfection (fig. 3).

4. Decide where some of your food will come from. We built a yard for cows and chickens so we could get fresh milk and eggs easily (fig. 4).

5. Think about where the patrons will purchase and consume the food prepared in the kitchen. How much space is required between tables? What kind of pattern is the layout of the floor plan? Is it a simple grid with tables and chairs in rows, or more free-flowing?

6. When you choose a name and create a logo, remember that even logos have patterns in them. The pattern of your logo can be based on size, color, shape, and name. Take care in creating your name and logo. Make both memorable! The best restaurants designers consider theirs carefully.

Fig. 1: In this design, the restaurant's exterior (a garden) and interior (low tables and seats) are part of the same open flow.

Fig. 2: The garden's rows follow a pattern: two rows of garden plants separated by dirt, water, dirt with dandelions, and sunflowers.

Fig. 3: Stock your restaurant kitchen with raw chicken, raw fish, wheat, sugar, and vegetables and store in chests. The furnace cooks food to perfection.

Fig. 4: It may seem strange to have animals near the dining area, but easy access to fresh eggs and milk make up for the barnyard feel.

ONLINE RESOURCE

If you want easy access to food, consider crafting an automatic egg farm. All you need is some redstone, hoppers, chickens, and a few other items. Check out this great tutorial on automatic egg farming: *http://goo.gl/08Oo6h*

Automatic egg farms allow easy access to fresh eggs without having to chase chickens around the Over-world. Build the walls high enough to keep the chickens from getting out.

MINECRAFT RESTAURANT DESIGN CHECKLIST

☐ **Choose a theme.** A few restaurant themes include fast food, fine dining, family style, and ethnic. Fast food restaurants focus on preparing and serving food quickly, while fine dining restaurants emphasize a custom high-priced menu. Family-style restaurants are casual and typically serve large portions. Ethnic restaurants have menus that originate from a particular culture, such as Mexican, Greek, or Italian. Try mixing up the themes to develop a custom restaurant.

☐ **Decide what kind of food you want to serve.** It can be diet specific, such as vegetarian, vegan, or chicken only. Perhaps the food is from a particular culture?

☐ **Design the space.** The space in a restaurant sets the atmosphere and pace. Some restaurants are dark with individual dining areas; others may be more communally centered with large tables shared with multiple dining parties. When designing the space, be sure to consider the route patrons and servers take when navigating the restaurant.

☐ **Choose an ambience or atmosphere.** High ceilings make the space feel large, airy, and often cold. Smaller spaces can make a restaurant feel cozy, encouraging patrons to sit closely.

☐ **Build the kitchen, dining room, and bathrooms.** Each space requires specific features. Imagine you are using the space as the chef or a patron. Consider how far the chef must travel to complete a dish or how smooth it is for patrons to find their table.

☐ **Build a menu.** Before your patrons get to experience your restaurant they will want to know what food you serve. Pay close attention to the food on your menu.

☐ **Craft a name and logo.** Some restaurants are named after the founder; others might be named after the style of food they serve.

Grow a Garden

Plants in Minecraft act similarly to plants out of the game. Both require sufficient sunlight, water, and prepared soil. Both start from seeds and, when harvested, give seeds in return. Plants outside the game use photosynthesis to produce their own food from sunlight. Plants in the game also require sunlight to grow. The farther your plants are from water, the slower they grow. As an example, wheat takes about 40 minutes of gameplay to grow from seed to harvestable crop. Of course, there are ways to make your crops grow faster, in and out of the game.

In this lab, you'll grow plants in and out of the game as a way to connect gameplay with real life.

Family Activity: Planting Seeds

Help your Minecraft-loving counterpart learn about growing plants in this family activity. Pick out seeds appropriate for the growing season, plant them, and observe them as they grow. Try experimenting with different seeds, soil, and water content. Take some time to garden. Whether you're planning a new garden or maintaining an existing one, this lab offers the chance to spend time outdoors.

■ **APPROXIMATE TIME TO COMPLETE**
  30 minutes

■ **MATERIALS**
  Pot
  Soil
  Packet of seeds
  Water

1. **Prepare the soil. Fill a garden pot with soil most of the way to the top. The soil should be rich in color and ready for your seeds and water.**

2. **Use a finger or a tool to poke a hole into the soil. Drop a couple of seeds into the hole and cover with soil. Water the seeds and place in sufficient sunlight (fig. 1).**

Fig. 1: Spend some time in the garden. Get your hands dirty by planting seeds in a garden pot, then give your plants the water and sun they need to grow.

Time to build a garden in Minecraft. Craft a hoe out of any material you have available. Use the hoe to prepare the ground for your garden. Once you've used the hoe, pour water within a couple of blocks of your crop. For efficient use of crop watering, place the crops in rows with water in between.

- **GAME MODE**

  Creative

- **APPROXIMATE TIME TO COMPLETE**

  1 hour in Minecraft

- **PLATFORMS**

  PC/Mac, Consoles, PE

Fig. 1: Craft a hoe using sticks and wood, iron, stone, gold, or diamonds.

Fig. 2: Craft bone meal out of bones. One bone gives you three bone meals. Collect bones by killing skeletons.

1. Potatoes, wheat, carrots, melons, and pumpkins are food staples inside the game. Potatoes can be found at automatically generated NPC (non-player character) villages and, more rarely, by killing a zombie. An easy way to collect wheat seeds is to break tall grass.

2. Craft a hoe (fig. 1). The material you pick will be subject to wearing down as it is used. Hoes are only for preparing the ground for planting, so you won't need to craft many for a typical size garden. Right-click on the ground to prepare the soil for seeds.

Fig. 3: The left row has been fertilized with bone meal. The other two rows have been left to grow naturally.

3. Bone meal is your secret growth-hacking tool. Bone meal can be crafted from bones (fig. 2). With bone meal, most plants will grow almost instantly. Without bone meal, your crops will take a few day/night cycles to grow to the harvestable stage (fig. 3). Gather bones by killing skeletons.

4. Once the crop is fully grown, left-click on the plant to harvest. Beware: wandering mobs can destroy your garden. Protect your crops with walls of iron bars (fig. 4) or any other block that will keep mobs out.

Fig. 4: Mobs can destroy your crops. You can prevent mobs from trampling them by placing iron bars to protect them.

MORE TO EXPLORE

Bone meal can also be used to create dye. Place bone meal in the center of the crafting table and a chunk of lapis lazuli to craft blue dye. Bone meal is an essential ingredient for crafting a white firework star.

Try your hand at automatic farming. You can use a piston system that drops water on the crops to automatically harvest all the plants.

The garden shown above was designed to promote rapid growth and easy access for harvesting. Because snow can hurt crops and freeze water, torches were placed nearby to keep them warm.

QUEST 3

Timeless Architecture

As an Architect and Designer, be sure to select the best blocks for the job. This quest is full of exciting opportunities to create and craft new designs.

LAB 5

THE ARCHITECT
Fortify your stronghold while crafting a castle worthy of a king and queen. Use any block in Minecraft and sugar cubes outside of the game to build your castles.

LAB 6

BUILT TO SCALE
Dig out a measuring tape to create scale replicas of your home. Start with a scale drawing on graph paper, then convert that drawing to your build in Minecraft.

The Architect

One of the most amazing aspects of Minecraft is the ability to easily design, build, tear down, and rebuild projects. Professional architects spend a lot of time designing a project before they ever see their designs built. In Minecraft, every player is an architect. Players plan, design, and iterate their builds with ease.

In this lab, you get a chance to experience building a castle in and out of the game. In the family activity, you'll build it out of sugar cubes. For building inspiration, choose a theme for your castle.

Castles have plenty of history that you can reference for inspiration for your build. We'll use sugar cubes for this family activity, but you're welcome to use any material you have available. Clay, cardboard, toothpicks, and even uncooked spaghetti are all great project materials.

■ **APPROXIMATE TIME TO COMPLETE**
1–2 hours

■ **MATERIALS**
Sugar cubes
Frosting
Cardboard
Spreading stick

1. **Gather the materials (fig. 1). You'll need plenty of sugar cubes (or other materials of your choice). If you're using sugar cubes, frosting works best as a glue; white glue can dissolve some of the sugar in the sugar cubes.**

2. **Build the foundation. Using a piece of cardboard as a temporary support is an easy way to build straight walls. Glue one sugar cube at a time and be sure to wipe up any excess frosting (fig. 2).**

3. **Every castle needs a tower. Here you can look out onto your land as well as station soldiers to defend the castle. Add extra sugar cubes to build the tower taller than the rest of the castle (fig. 3).**

Fig. 1: Gather the frosting, sugar cubes, and spreading stick.

Fig. 2: Build the foundation of your castle on a piece of cardboard. Be sure to include an entrance.

Fig. 3: Continue building the walls higher.

Fig. 4: Once you've finished your castle, you can use it to create a make-believe world with made-up characters.

4. **Castle towers used parapets, crenellations, machicolations, arrow loops, and other designs to protect soldiers as they defended the castle (fig. 4).**

5. **You can also design and build a portcullis, the heavy gate that blocks entry into the castle. You can always add a working drawbridge, or even a moat, for extra flair. If you're adding rooms to your build, add them before you add a roof.**

MORE TO EXPLORE
Windsor Castle, the oldest still-occupied castle in Europe, is in the English county of Berkshire.

In this Minecraft build, you get to claim your land and build a castle. Research castles to find your inspiration.

- **GAME MODE**
  Creative

- **APPROXIMATE TIME TO COMPLETE**
  2–3 hours in Minecraft

- **PLATFORMS**
  PC/Mac, Consoles, PE

1. Design your castle. Some builders start by drawing out their build on paper, while others go directly into the game to start building.

2. Build the first wall, which should be the front of the castle. From there you can gauge how big the remaining walls should be. Plan for a large enough opening for your entrance portcullis. If you build the walls five blocks thick, then you'll have space on top of the wall for soldiers to scan the horizon for potential threats (fig. 1).

3. Build the remaining walls. Some castles have four walls, while others have five or more. Build the remaining castle walls to your design specifications.

Fig. 1: The front wall is the best place to start your castle.

4. Design and build the interior. Build rooms inside the towers, and perhaps even a loft. Castles are like mini cities inside. All castles need a steady supply of food. When building your castle garden, be sure to make a water source nearby. Tip: Use bone meal to make the crops grow extra fast (see page 31). Use wooden fence blocks to protect your gardens and create animal pens, then spawn your favorite animals (figs. 2 and 3). Watch out—the chickens can fly.

5. Create a portcullis. Nether bricks look great as a portcullis. You can build one nether brick on top of another to fill the opening to your castle (fig. 4).

 ONLINE RESOURCES

There are Minecraft blueprints online for all types of castles, including Hogwarts from J.K. Rowling's *Harry Potter*. Here's a link to a video tour of an incredible Minecraft version of Hogwarts castle:

https://youtu.be/1ftVC8vNWAY

Fig. 2: Use fence blocks to create pens for the castle's animals.

Fig. 3: Plant your castle's gardens near a water source.

Fig. 4: Use nether brick fence to create a portcullis—the heavy gate that drops down to block intruders—with a dark look.

MORE TO EXPLORE

Work with redstone to design a working drawbridge. Keep in mind that your drawbridge may not work in the traditional manner.

 SHARE YOUR WORK

Once your castle is complete, share it with other players by inviting them to play capture the flag. Play in survival mode and make sure the tools players have are agreed upon. We suggest wooden tools because the game will last longer. The winner grabs the flag from the opponent and returns it to his or her castle.

Built to Scale

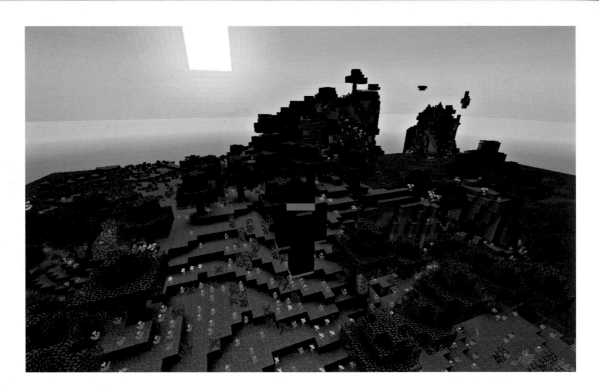

Scale is a representation of dimensions. Architects and engineers use scale regularly as an accurate way of changing the size of objects like homes.

In the family activity in this lab, you'll measure and draw a scale version of your home or room. In the game activity, you will recreate your home or room in varying scales. Try your hand at creating a smaller version of your home and a 1:1 scale where the measurements of your home are the same in and out of the game.

Family Activity: Sketch a Scale Drawing

Learn about measurements and creating scale drawings as you sketch a scale drawing of a room in your home.

- **APPROXIMATE TIME TO COMPLETE**
  1 hour

- **MATERIALS**
  Measuring tape
  Pencil
  Note paper
  Graph paper (see page 77)

1. **Dig out a measuring tape, as you are going to measure your home or room. You can pick a room or your entire home. Go around with the measuring tape to find the length of each wall. Start by measuring the longest room or hallway. Jot down the measurements on the piece of paper (fig. 1).**

2. **As you take measurements, draw an outline of the home or room. To draw to scale, you'll need to convert your measurements to a smaller size. An example is to make 1 foot equal to 1 inch. So, if your longest wall is 15 feet long, you'll draw a 15-inch line. Or, every 10 cm could be equal to 1 cm. (A 457 cm wall would be drawn as 45.7 cm.) Using graph paper will help you get accurate drawings (fig. 2).**

Fig. 1: With just a few tools you can measure your home or room. Jot down your measurements for easy reference during your build.

Fig. 2: As you take measurements, create an outline drawing of your home or room.

3. **Measure the length and width of furniture, such as couches, chairs, and beds. Be sure to include lighting, as you'll want to include appropriate lighting in your Minecraft build.**

MORE TO EXPLORE

Scale in art and design is often associated with proportion. Scale is the size of one object in relation to another, while proportion is the size of parts of an object in relation to the whole. The colorful snail sculptures below represent larger-than-life scale, even though all the snails are in proportion to each other. The Great Wall of China (bottom) is massive in scale as it is thousands of miles long, though in proportion to the Chinese countryside it seems small.

Craft your scale drawing inside of Minecraft using any block material.

■ **GAME MODE**
Creative

■ **APPROXIMATE TIME TO COMPLETE**
2–3 hours in Minecraft

■ **PLATFORMS**
PC/Mac, Consoles, PE

1. **Start by converting 1 foot (30.5 cm) of home to 1 block. Technically, a block is a cubic meter. We are starting with a scale version before we get to the 1:1 size of the home or room (fig. 1).**

2. **Using the 1 foot (30.5 cm) equals 1 block scale, build the foundation of your home (fig. 2).**

3. **Carefully go through the build and add walls and rooms based on their scale measurements. Once the walls are up, you'll be able to build a roof that looks like the one on your house (fig. 3).**

Fig. 1: Blocks in Minecraft are 1 meter cubed. Each arrow is 1 meter long.

4. **Add lighting, couches, beds, tables, chairs, and other decorative items and details (fig. 4).**

5. **Create a scale landscape around your home. Add new features to make your landscape and home the place of your dreams. Minecraft is great at visualizing dreams.**

ONLINE RESOURCE

One of the incredible scale models built in Minecraft is the starship USS *Enterprise*. The Taj Mahal as well as many cities and countries have also been recreated inside Minecraft. You can use Google Maps to measure a famous building and build a scale replica. Once you're on the map, right-click to see the "measure" option. Click on the map and a measurement line will appear. Consider measuring and building a scale model of the Eiffel Tower. Here's a link to the Google map with measurements: *https://goo.gl/GflClT*

Fig. 2: Start by building your house's foundation.

 SHARE YOUR WORK

Share your build with the world by taking screenshots of your Minecraft home. Publish it online and use the hashtag *#minecrafterbook* when sharing.

Fig. 3: Add a roof once you've built the walls.

Fig. 4: The interior of this simple house includes chairs, a couch, and bookshelves.

QUEST 4

The Arts

In this quest, explore blocks of various colors, textures, and styles. Create museum space and add to it a sculpture and a stage for performances.

LAB 7

CREATING FIGURES
Create a paper model of your favorite Minecraft character and then sculpt
yourself or a family member using blocks.

LAB 8

SETTING THE STAGE
Become a puppeteer and light up a stage, then take a passage from a
favorite story or movie, build the set, and perform it.

Creating Figures

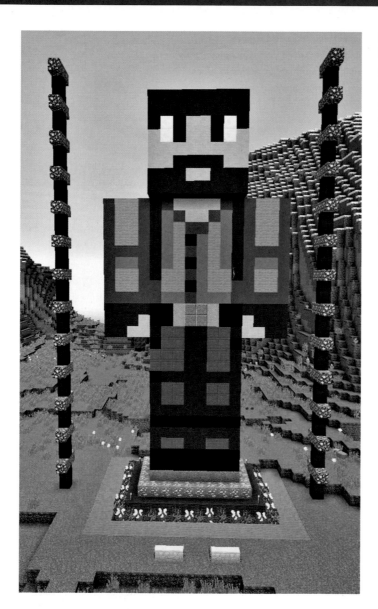

In the game, you and your family will work together to design a museum or cultural center that you can use for the entire quest. Throughout the space, you'll need enough room for statues on pedestals, paintings in frames, a stage for performance, and a hall for music.

In the family activity, you'll create a model of your character, or that of a favorite Minecraft player, to place in your museum. Parents may want to create a custom skin for their character prior to beginning.

Family Activity: Make a Foldable 3-D Paper Character

For this hands-on activity, everyone will be creating their own 3-D version of their character, or that of a favorite Minecraft personality, using the website pixelpapercraft.com.

- **APPROXIMATE TIME TO COMPLETE**
  1–2 hours

- **MATERIALS**
  Access to a color printer
  Scissors and glue
  Minecraft username for each
      character you wish to recreate

1. Visit pixelpapercraft.com and choose "Print" from the menu options.

2. Select "Print," then "Generators." Choose "Minecraft Character," click "Skin," and enter your Minecraft username. You'll see a deconstructed, printable image of your Minecraft character(fig. 1).

3. Print out the image and use scissors and glue to cut out and assemble the body parts (fig. 2).

4. Just for fun, you can also cut out and assemble the print version of one of our Minecraft characters (see page 75).

Head   Body
Right Arm   Left Arm
Right Leg   Left Leg

Fig. 1: Print out a foldable model of your Minecraft character. This one appears full size on page 135.

Fig. 2: Cut out and glue the pieces together to create a 3-D paper character.

Fig. 1: Design your museum on paper first. You'll need four exhibit spaces for this quest.

Fig. 2: Create an attractive pedestal. You'll need an 8x4 space to support the legs.

Your challenge is in two parts. First, design the layout for a museum with indoor and outdoor space where you can display your creations. Second, sculpt your character on top of a pedestal for all to admire.

■ **GAME MODE**
Creative

■ **APPROXIMATE TIME TO COMPLETE**
2–3 hours in Minecraft

■ **PLATFORMS**
PC/Mac, Consoles, PE

1. **Plan and then build the museum space and the pedestals you'll use to display your completed statues. Graph paper (see page 77) will be useful to designate areas of the museum. Future labs in this quest will ask you to add spaces within your museum to display paintings as well as locations for music and dramatic performance (fig. 1).**

2. **Locate a suitable biome in your Minecraft world that works best with your design. Perhaps your museum might hover in the sky or float on the ocean. Consider the location of the rising and setting sun, water features, and especially pretty views before building. Flatten out any area that needs it, lay out your floor plan, and build your pedestals (fig. 2).**

ONLINE RESOURCES

The Tate Modern Museum in London commissioned Minecraft builders and artists to create amazing interactive Minecraft worlds based on works of art in their collection. You can download these worlds for free by visiting: *http://goo.gl/Nvg2DB*

Fig. 3: Load up your toolbar and backpack with appropriate colors and textures.

Fig. 4: Build your sculpture from the ground up.

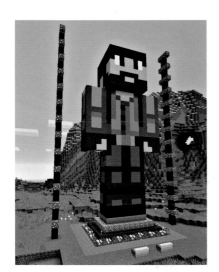

Fig. 5: Use glowstone to light up pathways and your sculpture at night.

3. Determine the size of each sculpture based on skill level. Beginners may wish to sculpt a bust of the head while more advanced players should recreate the entire body.

4. Use the 3-D character you created in the family activity as a model and prepare your palette. Choose blocks that closely match your character's colors and add them to your toolbar and backpack for quick access (fig. 3).

5. Sculpt your character from the ground up to eliminate mistakes later (fig. 4).

6. Add lighting (glowstone) to illuminate your masterpiece at night (fig. 5). Create walkways and viewing platforms between each sculpture.

 SHARE YOUR WORK

Share this lab online or in print by creating a collage combining images taken of your 3D characters with your Minecraft build. Be sure to include multiple angles and images of your work taken at night and caption each image. Use the hashtag #minecrafterbook when sharing.

Setting the Stage

In this lab, you'll first recreate a favorite scene from a book or story using Minecraft shadow puppets in the family activity. Then you'll take what you've learned and recreate that same scene or a new one inside your Minecraft museum. It's a chance for the whole family to perform under the bright glowstone lights on stage!

ONLINE RESOURCES

- Read about the legend of *The Butterfly Lovers* here: *https://goo.gl/YPX8Rc*
- For help making a shadow puppet, watch this video created by a professional puppeteer: *https://goo.gl/4RVGhI*

Family Activity: Shadow Puppets

To begin this lab, you'll make shadow puppets and perform a scene from a favorite story. Shadow plays have a long tradition in China and Southeast Asia. We were inspired by the traditional Chinese story of *The Butterfly Lovers*, considered to be one of China's great folktales. Like Shakespeare's *Romeo and Juliet*, the legend of *The Butterfly Lovers* is about two tragic lovers.

Fig. 1: Sketch your character before cutting it out.

Fig. 2: Attach each puppet to a stick with tape.

■ **APPROXIMATE TIME TO COMPLETE**

1–2 hours

■ **MATERIALS**

A short story with enough characters for each family member

Construction paper in a dark color, such as black or brown

Scissors

Tape

Long sticks

Focused light source, such as a small spot lamp or bright flashlight

Fig. 3: Perform your play by casting your puppets' shadows onto a wall or other surface.

1. Everyone will create a character from the scene you've selected. Sketch the outline of the character on the black construction paper. Use Minecraft-inspired mobs and characters, or create original puppets to tell your story. We created butterflies to represent our characters (fig. 1).

2. Cut out each character and tape it to the long stick to make it come alive (fig. 2).

3. Traditionally, shadow plays involve a thin, light-colored fabric on which the puppeteers project their puppets' shadows from behind. You'll need to hang a sheet if you wish to perform your play this way; otherwise, you can project your story from the front onto a blank wall using a focused light source (fig. 3).

Using Minecraft to animate short stories is widely popular. Kids and adults are producing and sharing thousands of hours of original stories they create in Minecraft on YouTube. In this part of the lab, you'll take a scene from a story or movie that you like, build replica sets, write dialogue, perform, and record the scene before posting it on YouTube.

Before you start, take a few moments to watch the video by YouTuber Adam Clarke, a.k.a. Wizard Keen, called *When Stampy Came to Tea*, a retelling of the story *When Tiger Came to Tea* by Judith Kerr (see the link opposite).

- **GAME MODE**
  Creative

- **APPROXIMATE TIME TO COMPLETE**
  2–3 hours in Minecraft

- **PLATFORMS**
  PC/Mac, Xbox, PlayStation, PE

Fig. 1: Using a storyboard lets you see what each scene will look like before you film it.

Fig. 2: Create a stage for your performance and dress it with items from your inventory.

1. **Decide on a short scene to recreate. It should be under five minutes. Before filming any scenes of a movie, directors draw a quick and simple sketch of what they want each scene to look like using paper (fig. 1). A movie where the camera angle never changes can be boring. By changing the position of your camera, your viewers will get a different perspective of the action.**

2. **Now that you know what you need your set to look like, it's time to build it into your museum complex. Consider building it outdoors and turning it into a proper theater, but not too far away from the music hall and sculpture garden (fig. 2). If you need help, check out the link found opposite to get a behind-the-scenes look at *When Stampy Came to Tea*.**

3. **Write the dialogue for each character in the scene and have each player practice reading aloud. Your script might look something like this:**

   Villager: Have you been to our village before, Witch Claire? It seems I recognize you.

   Witch: Thank you for asking me to tea. Even though I have flown by often, I've never actually visited this village before.

   Villager: Perhaps we met somewhere else. Have you ever been to Mushroom Park near Middlebury? I am a regular visitor. I collect mushrooms there for my stew.

Fig. 3: Rehearse to determine your camera angles.

Fig. 4: Dig yourself a hole and hop in it to get a more interesting camera angle.

4. Rehearse the scene with all the actors and determine the camera angles you'll use (fig. 3).

5. It's time to film the scene (fig. 4). Refer to page 11 for tips on filming or screencasting your video.

6. When you've completed your video, it may need a bit of editing. If that's the case, you can edit it after you upload to your YouTube channel. Use the video editor (see page 11) to combine your scenes, add music and titles, and publish your masterpiece.

ONLINE RESOURCES

- Adam Clarke is a very talented Minecraft YouTuber. To see his movie *When Stampy Came to Tea*, check out this link: *https://goo.gl/BEssTn*
- After Adam finished producing *When Stampy Came to Tea*, he wanted to share how he created the video in hopes of inspiring others to do the same. To learn how to tell a story using Minecraft, watch his video: *https://goo.gl/2PYeKp*

MORE TO EXPLORE

For players looking for a bit more of a challenge, consider these options:

- Film multiple scenes.
- Design scenes that involve advanced redstone use.
- Create an action adventure with special effects and TNT explosions.
- Add custom skins for costumes, and try different voices or accents.

SHARE YOUR WORK

Post your completed video on your YouTube channel and share it online using the hashtag *#minecrafterbook*

Game Design

Use Minecraft to create two games that each family member can take part in.

LAB 9

FIRE AWAY!
Create a bow and arrow using cotton swabs and then take close aim at your Minecraft target and try to beat your opponent's high score.

LAB 10

ABANDON SHIP!
Set sail for family adventures with a cork boat race. In Minecraft, who will be the first to captain his or her boat through the rapids filled with obstacles?

Fire Away!

Players have been using the mechanics of Minecraft to craft highly creative and interactive games ever since the game first came out. This lab asks your team to work collaboratively to create arcade- or carnival-style games using Minecraft. In the family activity, you'll create a target shooting game using a bow and arrows you craft from cotton swabs and Popsicle sticks, then you'll build a mini archery game in Minecraft.

This mini bow and arrow set is inspired by a project on the Brooding Hen blog (*http://goo.gl/P4Tor*). After everyone creates his or her own set, it's off to the range to see who the best shot is.

■ **APPROXIMATE TIME TO COMPLETE**
  1 1/2 – 2 hours

■ **MATERIALS**
  Sharp knife
  Popsicle sticks
  Dental floss
  Scissors
  Cotton swabs

1. Using the knife, cut four notches near the ends of the Popsicle stick, two on each end, directly opposite one another (fig. 1).

2. Submerge the Popsicle stick in water for at least an hour to make it pliable (fig. 2).

3. Wrap and tie the dental floss tightly first around two notches at one end of the stick. Carefully pull the floss taut, bending the stick in the process to create a bow shape. Tie the floss off on the notches at the opposite end of the stick (fig. 3).

Fig. 1: Cut out two notches at both ends of the Popsicle stick.

Fig. 2: Soak the stick in water for at least an hour.

Fig. 3: Tie the dental floss around the notches on one end of the stick, pull it to bend the stick into a bow shape, then tie it off at the other end.

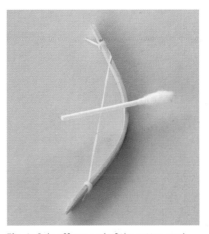

Fig. 4: Snip off one end of the cotton swab to make an arrow.

4. Snip off one end of the cotton swab to create an arrow (fig. 4). Test out your bow.

5. Load the arrow and fire away at a target or bowl and determine who the best shot in the family is.

Before you begin this part of the lab, find a location in Minecraft that meets the following criteria so you can build out the three games in this quest:

- A relatively flat area to host your archery tournament with good line of sight
- An open area where you can build steps high into the sky
- A sloping area or mountain nearby, to be used in creating a boat race through the rapids

The mini archery game you build as a team should have at least three different types of challenges based on the experience levels of the participants. For example, one or more might involve redstone and a scoring system. Another might be a simple series of targets set up at different ranges. Yet another could involve shooting mobs in the wild, in a gallery, or in another enclosed area. See the list at right for tips on using a bow and arrow in-game.

GAME MODE
Creative and Survival

APPROXIMATE TIME TO COMPLETE
1–2 hours in Minecraft

PLATFORMS
PC/Mac, Consoles, PE

1. **It's time to determine the kind of targets you'll be shooting. Stationary objects such as blocks, moving targets attached to items like sticky pistons or minecarts, or even random mobs provide good sport. In the example for this lab, we've set up three stations.**

   • **Activate the redstone lamp by hitting the wooden button with an arrow (fig. 1).**

   • **Collect points by hitting the center of each target (fig. 2).**

   • **Shoot at a redstone-powered chicken shooting gallery (fig. 3).**

ONLINE RESOURCES
Mini games are one of the fastest growing areas for Minecraft builders, with new games coming out all the time. In the multiplayer Hot Potato, one player randomly receives a potato with a lit fuse and must pass it along to another player before it explodes. You can discover more and download a version by following this link: *http://goo.gl/FeTnBQ*

MINECRAFT ARCHERY

- To launch an arrow from your inventory or when in creative mode, pull the bow back by holding the right-click button down until the string is all the way back and then release.

- Gravity affects arrows, so aim high if your target is far away.

- The maximum distance covered by an arrow is 120 blocks.

- You can pick up and reuse arrows shot by other players, but not arrows shot by skeletons.

- Use the flame enchantment to create flaming arrows that can blow up TNT.

- Arrows released at maximum bow tension cause the most damage.

- You can only move around at sneak speed if you have the bowstring pulled back.

- If crafting arrows in survival mode, you'll need flint, a stick, and a feather.

Fig. 1: Place a wooden button on a redstone lamp. Striking the button with an arrow will turn the lamp on, indicating an accurate shot.

Fig. 2: Set up target blocks at various distances and heights to test competitors' skills.

Fig. 3: As an extra challenge, create a redstone-activated shooting gallery.

2. Determine how your game will end. What will players need to do to be successful? Consider the following:

• Can there be only one winner?

• Is your game better if played with partners or in larger teams?

• Will you limit the number of arrows each player shoots?

• Will you time the game?

• Will there be any bonus point opportunities?

3. Now build your mini game together and play test it along the way. Need a few ideas to help get you started? See the suggestions at right.

SHARE YOUR WORK

Save this as a world file and post it for download on your blog or website. Don't forget to provide a write-up with the directions and tips for winning. Credit everyone who helped create the game and use the hashtag *#minecrafterbook* when sharing online.

STARTER SUGGESTIONS

■ Make players craft their materials or use dispensers to issue arrows.

■ To make it more difficult, set one of your challenges atop a steep hill and require players to make high arcing shots.

■ Build the world in creative mode and play in survival mode, where shooting mobs earn bonus points.

■ Use paintings for targets—they'll disappear when hit.

■ Challenge players to shoot while riding a horse or pig, or have them ride a minecart through each station.

MORE TO EXPLORE

More advanced players can research how to set up a scoreboard system and a clock for this quest to easily track each player's score.

Abandon Ship!

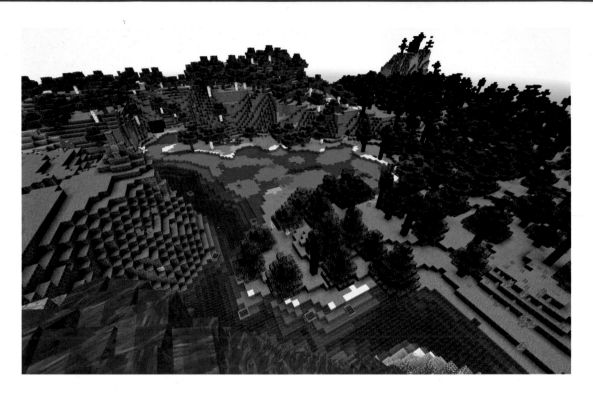

The second game you'll create for this quest will be a boat race between two or more competitors. In the family activity, everyone will create and decorate his or her own cork boat and race it across a body of water, then you'll build the course and have the race in Minecraft. Design a course full of obstacles like rapids, waterfalls, and slalom gates, which players must find their way around as quickly as possible.

Family Activity: Cork Sailboats

In this nautical adventure, you'll each design and create your own cork sailboat and race it around a challenging watercourse.

- **APPROXIMATE TIME TO COMPLETE**

  1 hour

- **MATERIALS**

  3 corks

  2 or 3 rubber bands

  Scissors

  Construction paper

  Crayons, markers, and other materials
     for decorating the sail

  Toothpick

  Tape

  Straw

1. Place the three corks together and use the rubber bands to secure them in place (fig. 1).

2. Cut out a small, square piece of construction paper and draw a colorful design on both sides. Attach the sail to the toothpick with tape and stick the toothpick into the middle cork (fig. 2).

Fig. 1: Secure the corks together with two or three rubber bands.

Fig. 2: Decorate the paper sail and attach it to the cork with a toothpick.

Fig. 3: Propel your boat forward by blowing air through the straw.

3. Race your cork boat in a safe body of water, such as a swimming pool, bathtub, slow-moving creek, or a rectangular tub filled with water. To raise the difficulty level, place obstacles in the way and require each boat to sail around them. Use the straw to provide forward momentum (fig. 3).

In this part of the lab, you'll build a watery racecourse and sail your Minecraft boat through rapids and down waterfalls to victory!

- **GAME MODE**
  Build in Creative; Play in Survival

- **APPROXIMATE TIME TO COMPLETE**
  2–4 hours in Minecraft

- **PLATFORMS**
  PC/Mac, Consoles, PE

1. Determine the length of the course based on the terrain you're working with and the skill level of each builder. See the lists opposite for ideas.

2. To save construction time, consider using a natural flowing river as part of your course. Incorporate elevated and depressed land around the river to make waterfalls, rapids, and small still ponds.

ONLINE RESOURCE

One avid builder known as TheNexusWarrior took on the challenge of telling the story of the *Titanic*, the doomed passenger liner, using Minecraft. Watch this amazing production here: *https://goo.gl/lVlqYØ*

Fig. 1: To place water, line up the crosshairs and right-click with a water bucket in your hand. Have an empty bucket handy to scoop the water up again in case it isn't placed in the correct location.

3. Build a meandering course so that several players can race at the same time. The finish line can be by itself, or the course can loop back upon itself.

4. Fill the course with as many obstacles as you'd like, but don't make it so difficult that you can't complete it in a minute or two. Challenging courses include sections where the water is still and where the water is moving quickly.

Fig. 2: Signs may be used as gates to create a short-term rapid and provide a nice boost in speed.

5. These are some basic rules for working with water and boats in Minecraft:

• Water flows eight blocks on a flat
space and will continue to flow as
long as it is moving downhill. Boats
will naturally move in that direction.

• Scoop water by right-clicking with
an empty bucket at the water source.
Place water by right-clicking a full
water bucket (fig. 1). You cannot
place water on top of water.

• Channeling water through "gates"
provides a speed boost (fig. 2).

• Placing glowstone under water
provides course direction at night
(fig. 3).

• A fountain-like rapid effect is made
by first creating and then destroying a
fountain (fig. 4).

• Right-click on a boat to hop in it and
left-shift to exit. Move boats in still
water by pressing W, but move faster
with a current.

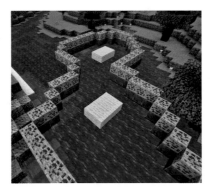

Fig. 3: A figure eight—created here with
strategically placed blocks—is always fun.

Fig. 4: To make a fountain, arrange stone
blocks in the water as shown. Right-click with
a water bucket on top of the tallest block.
You can then destroy the blocks underneath
without affecting the fountain.

SHARE YOUR WORK

Narrate a screencast of your race
and post it on YouTube. Don't
forget to add a fun soundtrack
and create a colorful title for the
episode. Be sure to use the hashtag
#minecrafterbook when sharing.

MORE TO EXPLORE

Here are some other ideas for
enhancing your course and the
racing experience.

■ Play in creative mode so players
can supply their own boats.

■ Automate the course by creating
a redstone-powered starting gate.

■ Instead of starting the race in
the boat, have players run or
leap to the starting line before
placing their boats in the water.

■ Place obstacles players must
maneuver through or around.
Squid make good obstacles.

■ Provide opportunities for players
to see and pass each other on
the course.

■ Create a shortcut or two, but
make it challenging to reach.

■ Include at least one waterfall.

Players earn bonus points by being
the first to complete a section of
the course.

Future Thinking

In this final quest, you'll use your skills from all the other quests to design and build your best work yet—a city of your own. This will be a new and improved city that is more useful and fun for its inhabitants. What's a city without a theme park? The sky's the limit—or is it?

LAB 11 **CITY PLANNING**
Tour your own city with an eye on the layout and locations of features. Then plan and craft a Minecraft city with all the best parts of the city you live in.

LAB 12 **FUN AND GAMES**
Visit a theme park, then create your own in Minecraft, complete with carnival booth attractions.

City Planning

The ancient Incas were known for their lengthy roads connecting their cities. The Romans planned their cities and roads to efficiently house their massive populace. The city or town where you live has its own design.

In the family activity for this lab, you'll analyze the features of your city or town. Then you'll sketch out a city you'd like to build in Minecraft. Be sure to leave plenty of room for the other lab activity in this quest. You'll get to design the city of your dreams!

Family Activity: Take a Tour

Grab a map of your city or town, either online or on paper, then use the map to explore its features and the way it's organized.

■ **APPROXIMATE TIME TO COMPLETE**
1 hour

■ **MATERIALS**
Map of your city
Walking shoes

1. Using a map of your city, identify the different features that make your city a city. Notice the layout of different zones and the intersections of streets. Use the checklist at right to make sure you locate all its features. There are two key things you'll need to do when planning your Minecraft city: take inventory, and analyze that inventory.

2. Walk around your city, analyzing it. Walk from your house to the school, or from the library to the police station. Look at the streets and buildings. A walking tour will help you gather information as you work toward designing your ideal city in Minecraft.

3. Pick a Minecraft map for your in-game city. As with any design, you need to know about the site of your build before you can create it. If you're picking a flat map, for example, then plan anything you want; if you're planning a random-generated world, then you'll need to anticipate traveling over hills and through water.

4. Sketch out your ideal city on paper or digitally. Most cities are divided into zones or districts for business, residences, schools, industry, and agriculture.

5. Decide how far people in your city will have to travel to purchase groceries, receive help from the fire department, and get to school, among other things.

CITY PLANNING CHECKLIST
- ☐ Apartments
- ☐ Auto mechanic
- ☐ Community garden
- ☐ Courthouse and jail
- ☐ Fire department
- ☐ Grocery store
- ☐ Hospital
- ☐ Library
- ☐ Open space
- ☐ Police department
- ☐ Recreation areas (park, beach, waterslides)
- ☐ School
- ☐ Suburbs
- ☐ Tall business buildings

In the family activity, you identified the necessary parts of a city, so now it's time to work together to craft your ideal city. An ideal Minecraft city will likely have a few extra features. Consider building your city in the sky or under water. If you plan to play in your city in survival mode, then you'll want to include abandoned mineshafts and monster traps. If you include teleport blocks, it'll be even easier to travel from the far ends of your city.

■ **GAME MODE**

Creative and Survival

■ **APPROXIMATE TIME TO COMPLETE**

2–3 hours in Minecraft

■ **PLATFORMS**

PC/Mac, Consoles, PE

Fig. 1: Start your build with a layout.

1. Choose a flat world or a random seed, or use a map you've been working on. You'll need plenty of space and topography to match your ideal city. We created a city layout before attempting our build. The colored wool blocks represent zones within the city. The template makes it easier for others to help build (fig. 1).

2. Fly around your world and start the outline. The outline should include the different zones for your city. Once you have the outline planned inside of the game, switch to survival mode. In survival mode you'll find out how far each of the zones and important features are in your city.

Fig. 2: This garden has wildflowers and a fountain.

Fig. 3: A fancy apartment loft decorated with expensive art and a great view of the city.

MORE TO EXPLORE

Regular elevators do not exist in Minecraft. Instead, you can build an elevator shaft and pour water down from the top. The water column can double as a liquid elevator that allows you to swim up.

Fig. 4: This large office building includes cubicles for employees. All it needs are villagers to roam the halls looking busy.

3. The manner in which you build is up to your style. You may want to start with the large buildings or the important city features first, and then fill in areas with a garden (fig. 2), residences (fig. 3), and businesses (fig. 4). This is one of those builds that could be never-ending. Allow your build to evolve, as you'll want your city to change.

 SHARE YOUR WORK

Share your city with other Minecraft players. Invite them to take up residence or help build out sections of the city. With the help of others, your build will become even better. Publish it online and use the hashtag *#minecrafterbook* when sharing.

Fun and Games

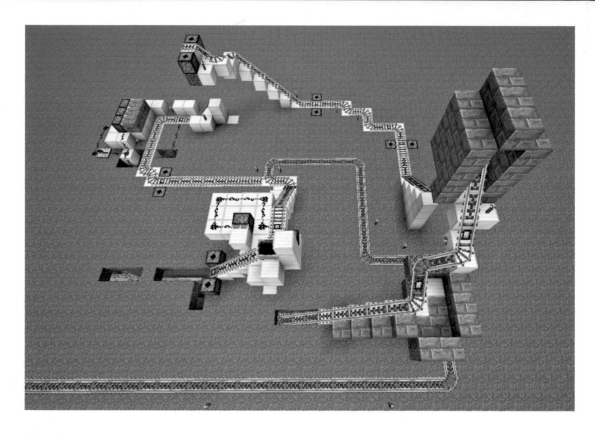

Some of the best cities have theme parks and carnivals. Whether there is a traveling carnival nearby or you are lucky enough to live close to a major theme park, you'll have an excuse to visit one in the family activity portion of this lab. In game you'll craft a theme park that fits your city and culture. Dream big.

Family Activity: Theme Park

This family activity is a great reason to purchase tickets and head off to a carnival or theme park. While there, you'll want to grab a map for later reference.

■ **APPROXIMATE TIME TO COMPLETE**
  8 hours

■ **MATERIALS**
  Tickets to a theme park or carnival
  Theme park map

1. While visiting the theme park or researching it online, pay attention to the types of attractions and the layout of the park. Take some time to study the map (fig. 1).

2. Spend some time sketching your theme park. Plan from the ticketing and entrance all the way through to the rides and carnival-type booths. Do you have a rail system to make for quick transport? Which rides greet you upon entrance and which rides are all the way in the back of your park? Do you have space for parades and for onlookers to watch the fireworks?

Fig. 1: Be sure to look at a park's map, whether you visit it in person or check it out online.

 ONLINE RESOURCES
If you can't visit a carnival or theme park in person, take a look online at what several different theme parks have to offer.

MORE TO EXPLORE
It's a great conversation starter to ask your fellow Minecraft players what types of attractions theme parks should have. This will help get your imaginations flowing.

It's time to dream up some new amusement rides—in this Minecraft activity, you'll get to build them.

■ **GAME MODE**

Creative

■ **APPROXIMATE TIME TO COMPLETE**

3+ hours in Minecraft

■ **PLATFORMS**

PC/Mac, Consoles, PE

ONLINE RESOURCES

- There are lots of videos on theme parks in Minecraft, even one called Notchland. Notchland is a sort of theme park with Markus Persson ("Notch") as the theme.

- If you included a maze in your theme park, be sure to check out The Maze Runner Minecraft video: *https://youtu.be/sVOxf3HdK4o*

Fig. 1: Build an archery course as part of your theme park.

1. Set aside a large chunk of your city and begin building your theme park. Create the attractions you sketched in the family activity and add on others if you like. Here's a list of fun Minecraft carnival attractions to inspire you:

• **Archery course. Place wooden buttons as the bull's-eye that activates a redstone lamp (fig. 1)**

• **Bumper boats using a pool of water and boats (fig. 2)**

• **Funhouse with command blocks and redstone features**

• **High dive. Build a tower with a small pool of water at the bottom. Jump from the top, aiming for the pool.**

• **Ice skating rink. Add villagers to make this even sillier.**

• **Maze**

• **Mini-golf course**

• **Parkour obstacle course**

• **Petting zoo**

• **Pig race with saddles**

• **Roller coaster (fig. 3). Don't limit your coasters to what's possible in the real world. In Minecraft your coaster can even drop from one rail onto another without causing any physical damage.**

• **Stationary Ferris wheel. Although it can't move it will look at home at the park.**

• **Waterslide. Craft a tower several blocks up. From the tower build wide steps. Leave enough space at the top and bottom for a pool of water. To start your waterslide, fill the upper pool enough to overflow down the wide steps.**

MORE TO EXPLORE
Build a rail around your theme park using redstone rails. Make it extra fun by building it through caves and mountains and on a beach. Install oversized creatures to spice up the ride.

Fig. 2: Bumper boats are easy to make and fun to play. The first person to break his or her boat loses.

Fig. 3: No coaster is complete without the large buildup.

2. Every theme park also has a series of booths, such as a ring toss and a milk jug throw. These are some Minecraft carnival challenge booths you may want to include in your build:

• Ring toss. Place a weighted pressure plate and toss blocks onto the pressure plate. Once enough blocks have activated the pressure plate, a piston lifts up.

• Ball bounce. Place a slime block on the ground, toss yourself on the block, and try to land in a designated area.

• Dunk tank. Have another player stand on a trapdoor. Shoot arrows at a wooden button to make the trapdoor release, making the player fall into a pool of water.

• Speed mining booth. Build a wooden wall ten blocks deep with the last block as a stone of your choice. Give each player a wooden pickaxe. The first person to collect the final block wins.

Lab Connections to Next Generation Science Standards

Lab Number and Title	Featured Education Concept(s)	NGSS (Next Generation Science Standards) www.nextgenscience.org
1 Do You Mine?	Scarcity, geology, materials engineering	K-2 and 3-5 Engineering Design
2 Fire When Ready!	Physics, chemistry, design	MS-PS1-4 Develop a model that predicts and describes changes in particle motion, temperature, and state of a pure substance when thermal energy is added or removed.
3 Please Be Seated	Culinary arts, service design	3-5-ETS1-1 Engineering Design. Define a simple design problem reflecting a need or a want that includes specified criteria for success and constraints on materials, time, or cost.
4 Grow a Garden	Botany, landscape design, biology	3-LS1-1 Develop models to describe that organisms have unique and diverse life cycles but all have in common birth, growth, reproduction, and death.
5 The Architect	Architecture, history, scale	4-ESS3-2 Generate and compare multiple solutions to reduce the impacts of natural Earth processes on humans.
6 Built to Scale	Scale, math, ratios	MS-LS1-1 Conduct an investigation to provide evidence that living things are made of cells; either one cell or many different numbers and types of cells.
7 Creating Figures	Design, art, history	1-LS1-1 Use materials to design a solution to a human problem by mimicking how plants and/or animals use their external parts to help them survive, grow, and meet their needs.
8 Setting the Stage	Music, vibration	1-PS4-3 Plan and conduct investigations to determine the effect of placing objects made with different materials in the path of a beam of light.
9 Fire Away!	Energy, competition	4-PS3-4 Apply scientific ideas to design, test, and refine a device that converts energy from one form to another.
10 Abandon Ship!	Buoyancy, hydrology	2-ESS2-2 Develop a model to represent the shapes and kinds of land and bodies of water in an area.
11 City Planning	Urban planning, design, human impact	K-ESS3-3 Communicate solutions that will reduce the impact of humans on the land, water, air, and/or other living things in the local environment.
12 Fun and Games	Recreation, tourism, electricity	MS-PS3-4 Plan an investigation to determine the relationships among the energy transferred, the type of matter, the mass, and the change in the average kinetic energy of the particles as measured by the temperature of the sample.

SCAVENGER HUNT CHECKLIST

☐ Apple	☐ Flower pot	☐ Pumpkin pie
☐ Bed	☐ Flowers	☐ Saddle
☐ Boat	☐ Furnace	☐ Sand
☐ Bow and arrow	☐ Gold	☐ Shovel
☐ Bread	☐ Glass	☐ Sign
☐ Cactus	☐ Grass	☐ Spider eye
☐ Cake	☐ Gravel	☐ Sponge
☐ Carpet	☐ Hoe	☐ Stairs
☐ Carrot	☐ Ice or snow	☐ Sticks
☐ Coal or charcoal	☐ Iron	☐ Stone
☐ Cobweb	☐ Ladder	☐ String
☐ Compass	☐ Leather	☐ Sugar
☐ Clay	☐ Leaves	☐ Tree
☐ Diamond	☐ Melon	☐ Vines
☐ Dirt	☐ Milk	☐ Water bottle
☐ Egg	☐ Music disc	☐ Water bucket
☐ Emerald	☐ Obsidian	☐ Wheat
☐ Fish	☐ Painting	☐ Wood plank
☐ Fishing rod	☐ Pickaxe	☐ Wool

Head

You can use the grey tabs to join the arms onto the body.

Pixel Papercraft
http://pixelpapercraft.com

LAB
7

Right Arm

Left Arm

Right Leg

Left Leg

Body

ACKNOWLEDGMENTS

Foremost, we would like to thank our families and express our deepest gratitude for their support and assistance throughout the process of writing this book. Without their love, creative ideas, and enthusiastic assistance, this book would not be what it is.

About the Authors

JOHN MILLER lives in Paso Robles, California, and holds multiple and single-subject credentials in history and science. He has been a middle school teacher for more than twenty years and has taught every subject in grades 6 through 8. He also holds a master's degree in educational technology and instructional design from San Diego State University and is a Google for Education Certified Innovator, a San Luis Obispo County CUE board president, and a CUE Lead Learner. John is a featured presenter at conferences and workshops around the country. He loves teaching twenty-first-century skills to his students and his passions include student blogging, e-learning, Minecraft in the classroom, photography, Apple, and Google. John is a contributor to *Minecraft in the Classroom* (Peachpit Press, 2014).

CHRIS FORNELL SCOTT is the founder and executive director of Woven Learning and Technology, a California nonprofit that runs Minecrafter Camps. One of his life goals is to inspire kids to dream big. In 2016, he moved onto a sailboat with his wife, three boys, and a beagle. You can find out more about Chris and his family at www.secretwateradventure.com.

Resources

Adam Clarke YouTube Channel
youtube.com/user/adamgorgeous

Creative Commons Music
http://creativecommons.org/legalmusicforvideos

Egg Farming
http://goo.gl/08Oo6h

Hot Potato Game
http://goo.gl/FeTnBQ

John Miller's Blog
http://minecraft.edtecworks.com

Minecraft
minecraft.net

MinecraftEdu
minecraftedu.com

Minecraft Wiki
minecraft.gamepedia.com

Shadow Puppets
https://goo.gl/4RVGhI

Tate Modern Museum Minecraft Worlds
http://goo.gl/Nvg2DB

The *Titanic*
https://goo.gl/lVlqYO

TNT Cannon by DanTDM
https://goo.gl/4Haq7A

When Stampy Came to Tea
https://goo.gl/BEssTn

Index